THE SKELETON
of the CROW

New & Selected Poems
1978—2008

SEIDO RAY RONCI

AUSABLE PRESS
2008

Cover art: "Glacier #2" by Brad Krieger, 1998
Oil on canvas, 41 x 29." bkrieger@neb.rr.com

Author photo: August Kryger
Design and composition by Ausable Press
The type is Dante with Cold Mountain.
Cover design by Rebecca Soderholm

Published by
AUSABLE PRESS
1026 HURRICANE ROAD
KEENE, NY 12942
www.ausablepress.org

Distributed to the trade by
CONSORTIUM BOOK SALES & DISTRIBUTION
34 THIRTEENTH AVENUE NE, SUITE 101
MINNEAPOLIS, MN 55413-1007
(612) 746-2600
Order FAX: (800) 351-5073
Orders: (800) 283-3572

The acknowledgements appear on page 203 and constitute a
continuation of the copyright page.

Library of Congress Cataloging-in-Publication Data

Ronci, Ray, 1954—
The skeleton of the crow : new & selected poems, 1978—2008
by Seido Ray Ronci. —1st ed.
p. cm.
ISBN 978-1-931337-43-4 (pbk. : alk. paper)
I. Title
PS3618.O6567S56 2008
811'.6—dc22
2008032812

The Skeleton of the Crow

From *Primitive Heart*

From *Under the Bo Tree and Versions of Ryokan*

From *The World of Difference*

From *This Rented Body*

The Skeleton of the Crow: Homage to Ikkyu

Sweet Homecoming

Sweet Homecoming

Stars shoot the heavens. Seeds.
Blossoms. Birds from the south.
A family walks away from the graveyard,
they still have far to go . . .

1

When I was a child, I practiced the act of dying
in bed. I would lie there, as if wounded
and terminal, breathe my last and shut my eyes.
It was easy and familiar, as if acting out
a recent memory. Something tasted
just the other day. It comes
and I feel fine.
A few good thunderstorms, blinding hail
cooling things off, rich green smell. Mist
in the valleys, the windows open
on heaven and hell.

2

After a few days up in smoke and delirium
I rise, sober at first, then just sad.
Someone playing Bud Powell records
fire escapes away, upwards of stench and trash,
through blazing sunlight on chrome, aluminum

and glass, this is what I ought to hear. But voices
of relatives and friends, memorized faces
and gestures playing skits in my head as I sit
stirring my coffee. "Shake it off!" I tell myself,
"Come on traveler, adjust, that's what you're
so good at." The faces, the chatter
panning and fading. I sit at the table
with my eggs and toast. Rooms are always filled
with ghosts, and some dance like longshoremen,
it's true. Death too, dances however and whenever
it wants. Why fuss? And yet,
art, god, lust and big business.
They come, they go.

3

In the fancy storefront windows of Cardin suits
and St. Laurent ties, Polo shirts and Bally shoes,
there's me: about thirty, in blue jeans, gumsole boots,
and a hole in my shirt pocket. What road
did I stumble on that set me one life after another
ambling over dirt through rising dust and sunshine,
neck and back sweat-soaked beginning to end
of day upon day? Poverty and simplicity
further back than I can remember.
One robe, one bowl, a pair of grass shoes.
The clouds fill my bowl and the leaves turn over.
I take my umbrella from my pack and wait
for the storm. A mother pushes her stroller
of baby and bundles quickly across the street.

Executives eat breakfast like dressed-up little
boys. I have no heirs, and nothing to leave.
When I die, a few will say, "He's gone."
And that will be the end of that.
You ask me, I ask you.

4

I don't know anything. But usually
I know too much. The rise and decline of opinions,
enough to brawl over; make and lose friends, and
the innocent.
But this cold September morning of rain and wind,
and the trees shaking it off,
and this warm woolen jacket from a brother,
and this umbrella from a friend,
and these pants and shoes on sale: I'm
a lucky man. And now this generous coffee
warming hands and body, the heavy sky above and
grey, I have only thanks. And don't
want to know anything else
right now.

5

And all these women I see and crave, what is it
in me that's missing, and turns my head with hope
to fill? I walk home through the warm,
sunset air, and the trees hush my footsteps.

I am content in my longing, knowing how
though satisfied before and again, I walk
some day or some night, alone with a cigarette
tossed to the gutter, my hands in my pockets,
the universe throbbing. The quiet. And I
am a sad, happy man in love with a world so stupid
it wants to always be right, and kill some
one or nation to prove it.
You can't usually help a lunatic
with his finger already on the trigger.
If you're lost and going to be shot anyway, enjoy
at least the weather and the memories of a few
good meals, a few friends, and all the lovely
women or men that got away.
Whatever is starved and looking
can never be filled
by a bullet in the head. I'm sorry.
I know people who want to change the world,
people for whom I have only respect
and great pity.

6

After the rain, laughter and singing
from a party far away. A neighborhood dog barking
and the full moonlight thinned by haze.

The raindrops on the branches glisten, the crickets
chatter. I am there beneath the pines,
where no one else has ever been.

Sunlight and birds wake me. Windless leaves
and the rats in the wall are quiet.

From last night's rain, a pond
cupped by an old, dry leaf.

On the grass beside it,
the seat of my pants slowly becomes moist.

7

The waitress leans against the wall with a smile
on glazed eyes changing with every thought;
various eyes ramming into each other, brief
shocks to the terrain. People smoking
their lungs out, drinking their bodies away: I
am not a holy man.
This morning I walked heavy with sweat
and uncontrollable speed, from place to place,
and my paycheck! Enough to pay debts, cover
bills, buy books and eat food! So thrilled
to sit down and eat food, to be served
and filled with food! Then
fat, I stand on the corner wearing wools in heat,
wondering where to drag myself, for what
spending next? And the legs are wobbly,
the palms soaked, the head snapping from side
to side, the traffic stuck, horns blowing,
Austrian waltzes on the tape machine,
cigarette smoke, the waitresses in red vests,

velvet dresses, puffed white sleeves billowing
through the terrace, holes in my clothes
but I have 800 times more money today
than yesterday and I'm spinning, nauseous
from exhaust, jackhammers, sirens, whistles,
faces, legs, manholes!

8

When I was broke, I came home, ate soup,
drew pictures, played the flute,
sat in meditation, and slept soundly.
When I got paid, I was hungrier than ever
and none of my clothes looked right. I sat drinking
coffee and eating plates of ground up animal flesh,
taking myself out for booze and strolling
by the river thinking about new shoes.

Home, and my nose would be running,
and my stomach tumbling, my phlegm tainted brown
and my asshole muttering. Too tired
to sit up straight, I roam the streets
and walk around eating a shrunken head
from the palm of my hand: it looks at me,
so I bite its nose; it talks to me,
so I spit out the eyes; it listens for me,
so I bite off the lips; it turns in my hand,
so I bite off the ears. What is this sound
I hear?

9

I am sad and tired, the reasons innumerable and
unimportant. What can I make today?
The globe is heaped with trash and a hurry
like my heart. My clothes
are not fancy and my belly not full.
My home is one flat pillow and a thin foam mat.
My hair grows long and out of style.
People let me know that I lack enough things
in life; they live as if immortal, as if it all goes
with them. I don't know
but the wealth of this sorrow of mine, and sitting
in the midst of all that goes on.
Today the sun is out but it rains.
Tomorrow, who knows? It may be
that the sun will shine only after
the rain and wind have stirred the path
before me. All I have left is this
embrace: for whomever,
for whatever.

10

Who's the Buddha coming off the mountain
when the ashes are cold, who says to himself:
I'll cook dinner,
I'll sit and drink the wine,
I'll talk well past midnight and make love
with the mountain in bed beside me.

I'm not asking who did it, I'm asking
who is "Who?"
Stretched out in her beauty, unaware
that I'm watching, I'll make the morning tea
and bring it to her in bed, then
run my tongue along the river bank.

11

There's no limit to the unnecessary, but
who cares? You have guards
protecting what your ears hear, sentries
standing by your eyes, hungry ghosts
sitting in your nostrils, slaves in your mouth
relaying only what the brain has edited.
The heart, what heart there is, sends
the blood around, with nothing else
to contribute anymore.
How could you think you're safe?
Prevent all you can, and still the bullet
for someone else misses, and finds you.
The punch meant for another face, finds yours.
The money they ask you for you don't have,
so they let the blood from your belly run
all over you! It doesn't matter
where you're from, who you know, or what
you pay in taxes.
When the flesh is torn apart
and the blood feathers fly, what's to hold onto?
Who's left to grope and grasp?

12

The flame of the candle shoots upwards, lightning
fills the sky, the thunder cracks
and the rain falls. The leaves fall
and the snow soon covers them. *Spring comes*
and the grass grows by itself.
These are the rules of the oak in the back yard.
The rain soaks my leaves, the sun bakes them.
Whether it be the wind or the love
for parents already dead, the oak
cannot complain. Cut it down,
count the rings, burn the bark:
earth, ashes, coffin and corpse.
We make love, we play music and dance,
we make families and write poems,
and when we drop anchor to thoughts
we make wars and cremations.
Whatever I say
is only more fuel for the flame
that consumes us.

13

I raise the collar on my jacket
and my breath makes smoke.
The train tracks sparkle with dew.
At this hour, only my boot steps
and the pigeons taking off.

14

The wind eases the curtain from my window.
That's the message from the earth.
And then, a cricket sounds.
Ex-lovers are nestled elsewhere. The dead
are somewhere cozy. The phone remains silent
and the traffic is thinned to nothing.
I have no use for anyone's opinions.
No justification is needed. No community.
No sadder memories. No reason
to believe or disbelieve. No master,
no slave. No moonlight, no warrior.
The wind
eases the curtain from my window.

Passing Through

Back To Beg

From the womb to a lamppost and down
the gummy street, each step has a trash can,
has a wall with a window, has a pair of legs
rising from high heels, up and up
past the shoulders, past the rooftops.
Night, lit like a hand in the gutter
holding a match.

Silk on the back of my hand
as I reach between her legs
for the entrance to this world.

Like the roads themselves, the children
spread. The exit
is not to be found in dying!

High weeds swaying somewhere naturally,
the green remains undisturbed.

Tell me, on what street am I,
kneeling in the rain,
with my eyes open,
drenched?

Crossing the Water

Most of the years I have let the lights
and miles amaze me, let the lips and hair send
me over the oceans and back, let the legislators
of intelligence publish excuses for my repeated
seductions; for the graves in the war zone,
for the balcony and gazebo, the vine and venom.
I could not climb any mountains because
the smoke in my lungs and the glasses clinking,
the eyes on me; the dim, velvety
conversations kept me bound
to the leather wingback, the fire ablaze and young,
no reason to be other than young until
years pressed seed from blossom
and mother enjoyed fulfillment in flower
and flower to be.
This is how the glass reaches the lips
and the liquor courses. This, in every direction
goes as Holiness in sinner and holiness
as Savior. It is that which makes the gods
muscular with goodness, and the devils geniuses
of evil. It is that which maintains what comes
and must go, that change that keeps the world
the same people, the same gods and lack of gods,
the same fugitives and saints.
I am no thief. Nothing is, nor ever can be,
mine.

Remembering How I Used To Be

He cuts through a vacant lot
on his way to his room. A sign says:
This Space Available for Development.
High grass, broken glass
and dog shit in the heat, he savors
every step, grins
at the way the grass swishes
like a high-hat, keeps his jazz underpinned,
his bass walking. He whistles
a minor scale, tiny hands
like a small shepherd with a miniature flute,
he doesn't wonder
how long this lot
will be an amphitheatre
for what moves him.

Once.

Passing Through

To leave for the solitary streets,
the anonymity of the faces in the crowd,
the pure pleasure of being
no one and owing nothing; to gaze
upon the face of the sky
overlooking like a guardian, an ancient
intimacy.

The voices and motion speeding
through my ears, past my eyes: absolute
stillness: a breeze, the river;
unattached to limbs or leaves,
passing through.

Equality

for Lou

I applaud the garbage man
with his great red truck, inching
slowly in
and out, between
cars and buildings, low
trees and air conditioners.
Back and forth, back
and he stops. Climbs
down from the cab.
Examines the scene like a surgeon.
He draws a crowd:
a white-haired man in seersucker
Bermudas, plaid shirt, sunglasses,
visor and sneakers; and myself
at the open window. Diesel exhaust,
engine roaring, he slips
the metal arms of the truck
into the slots on the trash can
and lifts it over his head
dumping it behind him,
emotionlessly. Not
like a parent lifting their child,
or a soldier lifting his dead, though
doesn't it have to be
the same?

Kalypso

A cool night
with the one who sprawls
across the bed without a word.

She has taken me into her house, she bathes
and feeds me, she warms the bed
and asks me questions as if my conscience
could be so beautiful.

She says she loves me, and says
nothing else. We sleep like twins.

What else do I need to know?
And I do, wrestling myself into a sleep
that doesn't last.

I am arms folded in a chair at bay
with my eyes on hers.
I have slept beside her and loved her often.

And I don't know who she is.

Orderly Evacuation

The movement
at the farthest edge of the field
appeals to me. The middle
is a sea of heads, familiar hands, shoulders
and hair. I begin
running across. Skeleton
of green wood bending, my body
moves slowly among the others. Waves
and waves of hair. Voices
lifting and climbing
over and over
each other.

In every direction, ships
are being built. In every corner
the sky hums like a factory!

The movement at the farthest edge of the ocean:

stillness,
the Light!

Isolation

Homeless and dependent on the benevolence
of an ill world. Embraced and set at the table,
candle-lit, with bread and soup, and the disease
I can't avoid in everything I swallow, everything
I touch, everything that wants so much
to welcome me, take my hand and take me
to bed. The heavy breath of germs
turns the lover into a Beast, and I realize
once again, there is more to this temporary
passion. How insignificant to wallow
in the Isolation Tank with one lover at a time
who wants only what is best for them, though
dreaming to bring escape or home to my life,
when out there are a billion ears and eyes groping
for sound and sight, hands coming forward, bellies
bloated: no escape home for the homeless!
No choice, but to swallow and embrace the sickness
that bends one in half, brings tears to the eyes,
dries up the throat, and leaves one
choking and sore.

Intimacy

Unless driven by greed
to illusions of control, power and success, one
remains a passenger and watches the passage
with awe.

A flash of doubt
is hell!

Too tired to walk
but walking,
asleep and chilled, stars
intimately far, politely silent
not to embarrass nor be embarrassed. One
in spite of oneself, looking
for shelter, drags along
to be taken in,

to toss
and be tossed
someday.

For Kyozan Joshu Sasaki

He is a quiet man
and a volunteer.

He doesn't have to think
about what he does
or when he speaks. He knows

and lives the life I can barely imagine.
I listen

and keep postponing,
keep deferring the sounds
throwing my arms up and legs around,
making myself a jackass
on a cliff walk, braying
into my own ears

into the mountainside
hoping for a landslide
or anything else
to blame.

The Shaman

The old man walked in from the sunrise.
Pine trees walked in with the old man.
The mountain walked inside.
The coyotes walked in on the mountains.
The old man took a long slow bow before the flowers on the table.
And the pine trees and the mountains
lowered their heads, the coyotes bowed
to drink water, the butterflies flew in
with the old man; the squawk of crows walked in,
the brook sound walked over, the wind blanket
swept above the treetops.

The old man touched his forehead to the floor
lifting his palms upward.
The mountain raised its head.
The old man stood and the sky walked in.
He started chanting for the dead
and his face looked white! His voice
reached, and the caskets closed, faces
gone. And then the names disappeared, the memories
and I disappeared. Ashes
dropped from the incense.
The old man stood before the flowers.
The mountain, and all that filled it,
stood there.

Out of This World

How he indulges in his immediate
and temporary relief, his quick vacations
to nowhere in his life. His exit beyond
where the suit of clothes, woven of family,
friends and enemies has no place
in his wardrobe. An invisible man, gone
only to himself as he draws
on his cigarette, lifts his glass
to his lips, lessens his responsibility
and his sense of duty.
That's how he makes it
past the guards of his tasks in life:
he drowns them out, throws decoys
over their heads and behind them.
He goes away only to end up being dragged
by the arms and forcibly returned
by the strongmen who grow weary of his tricks.
Bored with his slavery, no solace
in his treadmill exhaustion, he rises
and throws himself at his work,
and steals when he can, those moments
out of this world!

At the Mirror

I am not who I look like. Whatever
the face means, whatever the bend of the bones,
my sins from the other world, my Abraxas
is what this amounts to.
I don't see it but in the grooming
which is such a short time, and there,
put together in an airtight space, is hardly
a reasonable facsimile of a thing in motion
anchored to disaster, disease, murder,
accidents. There in front of me
the conscience constructs its high judgments
and tortures with logic
the mind that made mistakes
through greed, fear and pride
and razed the city and temple, the pastures
and mountains. Nothing left
unblemished. Every gesture,
generous and empty-handed,
rejected under suspicion.

The Narrator Speaks To Himself

Switched on the light. Creaked all the way
up the stairs in the dark. Sat down.
It's only the story of a life and whatnot.
Lives, them, 2 a.m., a car drives by.
All my windows are wide open. Empty
beer bottles line the sill to keep the squirrels
and cats out. I hear footsteps. Someone
cutting through the alley sees me
sitting by the window with the light.
I look around at how few my books have become,
from several shelves to a tabletop.
A moth flaps, trapped in a spider web.
Another car goes by.

Understand me! The voice coming unbeckoned
and beginningless. Where else in the world
is it 3 a.m. and a man sits at his desk, listening
to sirens and the quiet, lighting a match for
candle and cigarette. Socks stripped off
and shoes askew, clean clothes left
in the laundry bag.
There's nothing I have to be doing now, he says.
I have no wife, no children, no pasture.
Maybe I could've made it, but whether I did
or didn't, where should I be? Where else
in the world is it 4 a.m.?
Nowhere.

The footsteps long gone. The stars, clear
and close. The bed means more to me than words.
Off with the light, out with the candle.

For Mary

My sister phones and asks if I'm getting anywhere.
I say my house is full of ashes.
I tried to burn the whole mess away.
I realized I would die. I wept
and put the flames out.
It was a terrible mistake.

So I took a ride. Long, by yards
by acres and acres of junk cars and things
not repaired but held. Towns
less than a quarter-mile long.
Dogs and more yards of junk.
So I came home.

I came home and moved away.
And now it's like being on the sea
because the trees cannot be seen,
because one sees only sky and hears
only waves in this room.

Outside, the light breaks up into clouds.
The smoke-like rain fills the eyes and windows,
glazes the empty arms of alleys and streets
held open and stiff. Mary,
it is five o'clock in the morning,
and I am definitely
somewhere.

The Face That Made It

One part of oneself remains
out to sea, unaffected
by shorelines, rocks or cold.
Never one step
into public light, eyes
attending with care or criticism.

Seasons bring the hidden
to intensity after years,
the cast of certain desires is shaped
solid and smooth,

and the self poured into it
produces the living flesh of it,
to face the face that made it.

The Living

How long till the stones expire,
till dust becomes animal
and the animal stands erect
praising and cursing the suns and moons,
the earth solid and liquid, earth of mist
and Shades?
There is nothing to own. Why
deny it? Now, not long
before the corpses count
for nothing.

It is the living, secretly growing old,
not noticing until a line here or there, a growth
that never goes away, a flight
of stairs and a necessary pause,
a pair of gloves, a hat, a high collar
and thoughts, thoughts piled
too many to sort;

it is the living growing old who,
not noticed anymore, live
as if each day is too long and overgrown, too
late and languid. Memories
crawled together into corners,
collapsing into summer sleep.

Stocks and Bonds

I have my shares.
Every day full of ghosts and erasures.
A few remain who live in fear
on their knees in prayer.

I have walked the linoleum halls
of hospitals, my psyche tuned
to those about to depart.
I can tell if the ghost is gone
though the heart
keeps pounding.

I have stood by and coached the dying:
Breathe deeply, more
deeply!

And so I practice
each day.

Simply Physics

If I were to go back
from whence I came would be Midair! not
born, but a cumulus accumulation up a gutter.
Mother and father totally opposite
buildings, the alley between them: me.
And I stay here on this planet as long
as the buildings keep standing.
Depending on the earth's revolutions, tides
arranged and rearranged, the sphere's meandering
vapors swooning and pleasing
up against each other's gasping, hot
and heavy headwinds take me out, throw me
around the tough streets tacking
cross-town, me over here over there
dividing, subdividing, multiplying
and subtracting my what of a billion specks
I would be if I were to go back
to where I came from: all over,
and over again; add and take away,
the buildings go, I go.

Single

After all the music, last call, last song;
after the woman who reminded me by the streaks
in her hair, of a former "ever after" who now
thinks of me only fondly when drunk, and then
takes it all back. The multitude
disperses out the door. A cop car
parked unlit with two cops scratching,
a few loud intrusions on their radio.
And this long, long blonde dancing
in every direction, low-cut blouse and
liquid hips, blows away from night, smoke-like,
hanging. And another woman rocking
from wall to wall and man to man, kicks me
gently as I pass her again, not taking her
by the hand or arm, my hand not behind her neck
drawing her lips to mine, lips apart, tongue
running down her body, slowly; we never
wake up together.
Long walks home. Long drives through deluminated
streets, and then turning into your hallway,
The Mighty Face carries itself up the stairs
like royalty, convicted
of treason: blank!

Gassho

(To bow with palms joined together)

If I could afford to give flowers, at least
paint the picture unusual colors,
never-before petals, if I could give you
the trees I imagine, or the house's song
of bending, of springing back; blue earth
under the moon's white light. The natural hollow
under black swaying bushes, the grates
behind the library where heat meets cold
and rises like a spirit! Crackle of dry leaves
in the dark morning. If I could give you
the quiet.
If I could give the absence of my headache,
the absence of my shivers, of my voice
walking under the stars, deliberating
to the invisible my drunken revelations,
my history forced to fit a song like shoes
too small; my city, a city of dead men blossoming
in steel, concrete names and dates, memorial
streets, commemorative squares, a man
antiqued, on his hands and knees, weeding.
If I could give the absence of these legs and arms
flailing in a dream of drowning or falling
through space. If I could give the absence
of a single thought,
a solitary ripple.

Return the Land to the Land

Left them all, and the innocence too.
No longer hopeful at the porch to be kissed,
on the doorstep embraced at the threshold;
the bedroom, a long life together, repeatedly
refused and walked alone, honest in tears,
loneliness and delight. Extravagantly sad
and seduced by my footsteps moist
on the silent field. I alone, inhaling the stars'
words, reading the lips of the breeze, the air
circling around me like a cloak,
my feet sinking into the earth, as my mind sinks
into uncontrollable night. Give it
whatever it wants, because it takes
whatever it needs: the pure animal, the complete
angel! I work and earn its rule, subdue
the slaves and masters of the senses,
level the kingdom to the land,
return the land to the land.

Music

Especially in the cold!

I sat in the Luxumbourg Gardens,
formal children in their dress wools,
sticks and sailboats; I sat
all bundled up in my arms, collar raised,
whole orchestras in my head, symphonies
lifting to the ceiling and going
out! and up! and up!
Through centuries!

Just like that.

Song of the Waif

After Rilke

No place to lie down and say: home.
I live here, work here, grow and reap here.
No place to send myself.
So in this cold night,
with a borrowed coat and a borrowed bike
I sit looking out the window
of a borrowed home and someone's wife.
And this body.
It gets later and later, and I wonder
could I come and lie beside you and trade
warmth for warmth. You sleep
and snore lightly. I'm afraid to disturb you.
What an old man I've become, startled
by the sound of my own shoes
hitting the floor; my own hands
coming to my face. I sit far inside
myself as if an empty station
where no one sweeps, comes or goes.
I am bold no longer.
What initiation, what test, what trial, for what
reason do I circle the earth on foot looking
for a place to rest? A voice
says: Don't move!
I stare at nothing. I cannot move.
I cannot weep or laugh. I no longer miss
a lost family, my tears no longer like a visit.
I have a little song I sing.
When I remember it, I'll sing it.

Ancient Trees

I have left them all, left them always,
alone as I have always been,
coming in then going away
to sit in the mountains and listen
to the smoke rising from the altar.

And they ask themselves
where I have gone and why
they are wounded.

The cities move skyward, and below
equally stainless steel and satin metal!
Sky, earth and sea take blows from fleshy hands.
Molten eruptions, waves crashing like buildings,
trees and homes shouted at, pummeled
ceaselessly by wind and rain.

Ancient trees on winter's hillside, the forest
is black and big-hearted. Each trunk
is a mirror into past and future;
each, as I touch and address it, tells me
what I need to know,
whether I understand or not.

Ready

I know my gait and shoulders are strong for passage.
Each moment learning the grace of the limbs,
the toning of a muscle, learning
the floodgates, the tempo of the river,
its quiet and rage.
I know my back has turned me toward this
departure with every departure. I am primed
with experience of the edge and flowers,
the sky above and below in the valley.
One step not taken:

In the darkest dirt around the trees, digging
by hand at the roots and rocks, under the freeze
of deep night; under the flames of a scratched
and bloody sky; earth ripped and made sterile,
dry mouths wailing for food and sleep.
The leaves on the branches change flags, alter
names and dates, hang heroes and saints,
seal the flesh on pages and march the streets!

Uncovering the roots, handfuls of black
earth tossed over the shoulders, piled behind.
Not stopping to look long and be distracted.
One purpose: to unravel the twisted, the gnarled
grip on the earth.

Primitive Heart

Peter's Denial

I, the one you call the rock, finding more ways
to deny you before the cock crows, wait
long hours, 40 days, 400 days speechless
to raise my palms to my face: "What is this?"
The food, the water, all the bodies dropping
from the womb, passing through these fingers,
I look for you everywhere, for a sign;
I feel the waves coming outward from your shore.

From the desert to the sea, the lesser gods
have made offerings of gold smoke and watery wine;
but only you are what I seek in their eyes,
the lines in their faces, their gestures
stretched across a canvas depicting the long,
ragged march, the intonation of cries, centuries old.

What I look for, what I keep seeing
in every picture I fill with color, is you.
The greetings of strangers amount to dust and disappear
like the hands that pass the moments, pass
the jewels from generation to generation filling
the starlit, crucified acres.

In the swollen sea, to want to hold you,
to want to speak words that become vacant, how stupid
to make passionate absurdity of lifting a pen,
lifting my head from the pillow.
I turn away from your grace to gamble and drink,

to visit the women and pay the high price
losing my breath in the spray.

In the world, I become the world.
Change the world, and I am changed!
Call me the rock that bleeds and blossoms,
call me the rock that too slowly turns to dust,
call me the rock upon which rocks are piled . . .
that what they should do to you
shall be done also to me;
that it is as fitting to murder a prophet
as it is to build a church upon a stone!

With all that you have shown me,
I must save myself.

Icarus

I ask the court if I was the only one
who ever misjudged the affection of others
and turned away, towards what I thought
and prayed, was the face of God.

How I struggled beyond my powers
to keep afloat, struggling more
as my wings fell apart
and the jet-black water raced towards me:

Had I only died in that fall!

The kindness of the farmers, their wives,
their sons and daughters, enough now
to make me weep; even then, the chance
to face God in the faces that found me!

How elusive it becomes, as soon
as the strength restored lifts me from infirmity
to rebuild with new materials the wings
that carry me above the earth.

Different lands have I fallen upon,
and arms and laughter replenished me.
With high blood and hard hands I refashioned,
after my father's scheme, new ways
to escape the labyrinth.

Yet always, when I have reached the bounds
I dare outreach them.

History does not remember me.
Like Cassandra, no one believes
that I have stood among them,
that I have said a word.

Unwept. Unburied.
The son of the Master Craftsman
lives.

War Memorial

Providence, R.I.

Grey slabs standing in a circle. New buildings
thrown up against a slate sky. Gnats
around the rusted green trash barrel
upon which someone has written:
            "This place sucks!"

It is 7:00 a.m., a Wednesday; the flagpole pulleys
bang against the poles, the breeze plays
with my hair and the colored tags on my suitcases;
rain-glossed leaves, puddles like black holes
in a hollow earth surrounding this tribute to life.

How many sacrifices must we offer to earth and fire;
how many libraries must we convert to pyres;
how many generations of children made bitter and sad,
blossoming to insanity? Made to squeal,
"What's in it for me?" we square off and glare,
pistol ready, eye to eye:
Burns, Burnside, Burrell, Burton, Byron,
D'Agostino, Daily, D'Alessio, Danforth, Daniello:
arbitrary names, arbitrary deaths!
        "Thoughtful men will be eternally grateful."

Only a "rational" mind could sit and thank the dead.
The heart cannot praise the crimes of a species that
knows better and turns away. Let no one say
you wasted your lives.

Helmeted men climb the scaffolding armed
with hammers and nails; briefcases pass by with people
attached to them. Buses unload, load and leave.
Dead men, soldiers: "This place sucks!"

Happy Hour

Beer 1
In the smoke-filled pastel lounge: pale, garrulous women on high stools with their drinks lifted by lush-painted nails to velvet colored lips; indecipherable music; men glaring at baseball, shouting and smoking, snap-neck to the women and back to the game: tallies, both.

Beer 2
High heels parked barside with her lips she looks at me, with her eyes she says something loud, like the music.

Beer 3
Smoke puts its arm around my neck or runs its fingers through my clothes. Six men surround a woman flipping her blonde hair over her shoulder; high black boots, skin-graft blue jeans.

Beer 4
The dusk walks through Indian summer's open door, purplish remnants of a disappearing sun.

Beer 5
Where am I in this picture? Neither fixture nor man.

Beer 6
Like a drunk who laughs, laughs at nothing, nothing known to anyone outside him, who passes street after street, city upon city, as if nothing, nothing ever happened . . .

Beer 7
Here today, here tomorrow.

Paris

He is standing by the bridge on the Left Bank
taking half a tooth from the ground-up sandwich
in his mouth, holding it up to the sun, disbelieving.

He is standing in the center of the city
that is the center of the world, and suddenly
there is no one in the marketplace!
His eyes squint through the light
and into the shade behind the columns,
beneath the porticos, to see if indoors
le garcon is loosening the cork
of a *petite liqueur petillante,* hands
pressing an apron down flat, a tie
screwed in place, a glance into the silverware
tapping the coif . . . to see if a woman
free from beauty and necessity can bring him
to disappear at a touch, as the song
returns to the bird and the wind, as the trees
return to the sky.

*(He has come from light-years before his birth and traveled
the circles of future lives just to be standing here in this flesh
quickly corroding, reflecting on its rapidly vague memories:
could that possibly have been . . . him? And the boundaries
between his actions and anyone else's disappear. In a moment,
everything he has loved or taken the time to hate, he has be-
come; with no trace of time or change he has never existed.)*

He stands staring at the half tooth
in his youthful afternoon by the ancient Seine.
The ripe sun like a halo lighting his hand
as he examines his kernel of truth,
his speck of warning from the body's angel;
his future on the planet
becoming brown and black
and no color at all!

Maastrict

Cold, clear blue sky; morning sunlight splashing against the brown, curtained buildings opposite my window; a car whispers up the empty, narrow street.

I awoke sad and nowhere; dreamless, no destination—but longing. For what, though? What could I ask for that I haven't already had for however long or short? Will I always breathe to want?

As the women of Maastrict parade their colorful beauty through the medieval streets, whole lives of possibilities flash across my imagination's embrace. Their eyes aimed toward some specific destination, focusing on some primary or secondary detail; they walk, oblivious to the eyes watching their every curvature of motion. The brisk air rushes up to brush them off, redden their cheeks, touch up the hair so that every step is fresh from the boudoir. Their high heels clack along the cobblestones. Bells toll in the distance. They are making their way, being replaced in their passage by the many, by the moments, that follow.

Someday, I will not breathe to see it. Someday, if I live long enough, I'll be too old to follow, will stare, tipped over my coffee, dressed in hard coat and high collar watching the world I knew and traveled go on without me. Those moments of liquor laughing smoke-filled eyes with tears, sore cheeks from hysterical belly-deep joy: the bright world pieced together by the dead, the going, the forgotten, the newborn: the briefest of earth's brief moments when all is in perspective, gone.

I will retire to an afternoon of warm sunlit wood deep in the yellows of a corner in a café, away from loud voices and pinball machines. And there, there I will dream other dreams.

Barges

Well, Holland

I sit by the River Maas listening to the birds and watching the few barges that glide east then west; cars pass by on the dirt road before me. I am the stranger, some people wave, some don't. The cows go on grazing.

Suddenly I hear coughing and a pounding noise. For once it isn't me! Two cows butting their heads together, the coughing cow already on its knees being pushed back across the pasture. Flocks of birds circle the far side of the river; another barge gone by, hardly noticed. The cows have ceased their dispute.

I think about this alien nature that surrounds my metropolitan corpse: it could almost be hell! The cries of geese, the chattering birds, the splashing swans, the crows cawing on the fence posts of the harvested field, the erratic flight of a lone swallow; a language that once held meaning, a meaning that someone understood, that somewhere someone still does. But I don't.

My ears are filled with reverberating sounds that echo the life of the city I left. In this solitude, the cow coughing is a world of dead and dying friends; the birds circling in huge flocks are commuters late and aimless; the blackbirds are arrogant overseers; the wrenching sounds of the geese and ducks are the indecipherable voices of a bad dream. One thin tree with 16 leaves has 15, 14, by the end of the day maybe none: this, I understand.

The cows move down the pasture towards the river licking one another. A barge takes pieces of the earth upstream, another takes the work of factories downstream: no barge comes or goes without cargo.

Song From the City Inside

I have been given food when I worried
that I would go hungry.
I have been given a place to sleep,
though I walked homeless and afraid.
I have been bathed and given fresh clothes
when I worried that I would smell and be dirty.

Once, I sat in the shade of a tree
with a loaf of bread and a bottle of wine,
and kept myself from sweating and anger.
No questions. No doubts. I was younger, and stronger.
The demands of my society didn't affect me.
But now, as my gravestone rises out of the earth
like a bush, and my epitaph is beginning to bloom on it,
I'm afraid I'll have no place to settle my affairs
and drift, willingly, into the next world.

Yet, the Sages have always said:
What are you missing? It's true!
When I was hungry you gave me food; thirsty
you gave me drink; sleepy you gave me a place
to rest. When I was crazy you gave me
the language of the sky to settle my anxiety.
But I lost, long ago, what I once knew.

Tired, weak and distracted, the world has moved
inside me, crowded with buildings, loud noises;
the pure light of the sun obscured by clouds,
the wind overcome by shadows.

Noman

Noman is my name. My father and mother call me
Noman, as do all the others who are my companions!
—Odysseus to Polyphemos

There were days I could run,
run for hours
through fields and streets, from hills
to steeples, forest to factory,
and falling in love,
burying the dead,
falling asleep
being chased, chasing
after.
And now,
it is no longer I,
but some other I watch
and feel pity for,
am amused by,
interested in, bored with,
intrigued by, indifferent towards.

Yet, still I go with him
through his rounds, taking him
by the hand, leading him
when I can, away
from an obvious danger.
He does
what he thinks he needs
to do. And I,
I help him with the rest.

Golgotha

Branches. A crown of thorns.
A shower of tears.

There rise
the fingers
of a millenium's worth of hands,
their bones washed up to the surface
like so many trees
crossing paths, so many
voices missing their intended,
heard and misunderstood
by strangers
sculpting new monuments,
new edifices of magnificent stature
founded on the misapprehended,
skyward, full of mythological muscle.
The celebration
of the slime and mortar man,
the banker making deal after deal
taking the lives of those who don't yet exist
and creating their futures for them:
everyone walking around out of a fear
that has no choice over its job: its life work
but to breathe and carry out.

The branches smack
against one another.
How is your journey of lies,
and how do you like this treason

that you pit against yourself,
a mutiny, a mutiny led by the self
disguised as another?
Disguised? See? So clever
that even you
think there are "two."
What are you looking at
if not your self?

Mary Magdalene

He didn't speak my language, or any language.
He threw no rope to lift me up, held out no hand
as I struggled on the edge. He kicked me out,
again and again: Climb up
on your own, if you can make it!
In the sea of no-distinctions nothing cherishes me.
And that's the way it is in this world.
If He's a teacher, here's His lesson:

No one can help you. Eventually you will learn, aeons perhaps, but eventually. Ask the question and already the Path appears. Only cease from right and wrong, from wise and ignorant, and go forward until the corpse no longer owns you. Throw away life, throw away death, progress and failure. Above all: do not be afraid.

To the follower of the Way, becoming a Master is not the goal. Every joy, every tear is more profound than the million volumes of scriptures. If you seek fame, glory and material success you haven't even left your mother's breast. The ignorant don't understand what it means to turn the other cheek; they can't comprehend the eye of the needle. They ignore the death and resurrection by thinking only of their bodies and bygone loves. They become their bank accounts, they become their clothes, they become their regrets. The world is never the same, and no one owns a thing, not even the soul! Remember that.

Lovers

*Lovers don't finally meet somewhere.
They're in each other all along.—Rumi

Anything I have worth having, I want to be yours!
Whatever song I hear, whatever music rises inside me,
whatever dance grabs my body and whirls it in circles
I want to be yours.

And the colors that gaze upon the earth and sky,
the minute alterations of each moment's seasons:
the earth churning inside the earthworm,
the flowers shifting in their beds, the sky
alive in the bird's wings, the ocean sleeping
in the fishes: all this
I want to be yours.

In the vast blue-black solitude of night
when the air's elixir explodes my past and future
and leaves me laughing in the starlight;
when I am no different from the geese and swans,
from the pigs and fishes, no different from the bell
and the sound of the bell, no desire
to be a king with a queen; there, in the clear
bright black above the mountains and below the rivers,
there I wait, to give everything to you.

It is not desire that makes me spend all day,
day and night, in the presence of your face.
Now that I know what it's like

to spend every moment with you, conversing
over the smallest details, I can never be far away.
This love has no weapons or rules; this love
has no purpose.

And when I feel the sweat pouring
from a hard day's work in the sun;
when I feel the chill of winter
shoot up my spine as I sit before the fire,
when I gaze back at my footprints across the sand,
when I see my tracks in the knee-high snow, then
the sound of my voice calling for you in the forests,
calling your name in the city, calling to you
alone in my bed—the sound of my voice
brings you to me!

I possess you without seeing you.
I make love to you
without touching you.
I grow old with you
without losing a breath.
Better to love you always, and remain alone,
than to love another
and embrace an illusion.

All that I have worth having
is yours.

Under the Bo Tree
&
Versions of Ryokan

Under the Bo Tree

1

Then most beautiful
just before grey clouds
roll cold at their trunks
bright red
soft yellows
through air dry up
crunch
become soil
these woods alone
autumn
the older
the more time
starting over
swallowed up
unfurling
in the wind
awhile
for years.

2

Dawn spreads
through the mist
the roosters
the bells from the steeple

the fog so heavy
a small rain
falls
from the branches.

3

The sky in the pond
rises to the sky
trees join the clouds
a man climbs out of bed
his body with clothes
sits in a chair
ties his shoes
his mind
sits on a train
mist on top of the reeds
clouds lit pink and white
traces of night still plump
a single bird flies beyond
the fading moon
then another and another
the man
opens the door
and by evening has forgotten
the trees
darkness
and dreamless.

4

Curve in the road
sun on its feet
net of branches

cold smacks the trees
faces lined up red
cobalt horizon

night leaving
the lawn white
embracing the body

the cold arms of the season
when the animals
disappear.

5

The dry sticks
dry leaves
the dirt
dust wind
amounting to moss
on the fieldstones

the sun whitens
the fronts of the trees
black line

on the back
the wind
rips the black
pond blue.

6

Frost on the field
white morning light
on the bleached barn
broken farmhouse over
grown gold weeds
soil hard and grey
steam on the sun side
of the tree trunks
not a bird
not a machine
but the silence
of one man
stopped.

7

Walking becomes involuntary

a dent in the air
a step away

from nothing where

all begins

as a need to say
"wow!"

under the stars
frozen

passing
right through me.

8

The cold
pushes the blood aside
howls through veins
to heart

from heart throughout
the limbs

hands and feet
frantic for heat

old hands
stretching from the dark
to the flame.

9

Inside is as tall
and cold as out
the wind empty
stays empty

the trees
shape a tunnel
black without sound
until the hill and bend
the pine trees
at my doorstep

there is nothing
in my house nothing
outside but the soft music
and the clock

a place to sit
and sleep.

10

After ten maybe twenty
years
of broken staircases
of rotten fire escapes
of headlights climbing the
walls
you have taken a hammer

and leveled the landscape
not with a single blow
but little by little
tapping away chip
by chip.

There is
a daybreak star
and a cloud forming northwest
to bring rain
wet down the dust give
seed something to grip
there is the quiet
heart beating and
the sleeper's inaudible
breath inhaling
the horizon
exhaling
the man.

11

Scribbles
on the off
white
sky
brittle
leaves
the size
and color
of pennies.

12

It's been a long
time since

this wind bright
sun a trace
of old
snow

squirrel on a fence
holding on
swirling

papers and leaves

walking
my hands
unfisted

in my pockets.

13

The new leaves
on the tree grown larger
through the hard
quiet winter
the thick trunk
lifting to light

spring breeze
caressing the arms
playing at shadows
older each summer
no longer
to be a house
by fall
to be a monument
a shelter just
eyes
all ears.

14

On the mountain the sun
inside me the birds travel miles
up and down the spine the coyotes
glide down from the shoulders
through the high grass
leaping rocks
drink

late night early
morning far away
back and forth
scratched voices
reverberating
flies crickets wild dogs
the ground squirrels' incessant chirp
scorpions asleep in deep dry dirt

breathing slow and quiet
wind up from the desert warm
branches holding up their kerchiefs

fly!

15

Today I knew
I had played
the piano well
when I walked outside
the birds
were still
singing
in the plum blossom
branches.

16

I play a blue violin with a paintbrush
while a bird sings on a pile of bricks
and a feather floats to earth forever

a boat carries gravel up to the city
and the river rises against the houses
there are eggs on the lawn
a prayer glides across the current
waddles over the grass and covers her babies
a small song while day turns the river white

slow in the midstream the river flows
against itself a boat carrying sand
from the city again the river rises

a young woman with her dog watching
from the edge of the dock eyes
filled with blue a baby in the carriage.

17

This house
wants its windows open
just a bit

the trees
and tall weeds
to waver.

18

Not one moment of illumination
belongs to me
the water laps the shore
the boat is gone
I hear the children's voices
the seabirds
the engine of a barge
a rustle of leaves
a page turning a silver stripe in the river

cold wind at my eyes
the squawk of a seagull
it is quiet again.

Small birds flying just
above the river's ripples
three trees whose branches join
look like one
bright green grass and ash black loam
a mother and her ducklings
I've seen it
and said so before
but that does not belong to me
the words
the images do not belong to me.

The cabin of the barge
is filled with flowers
the water is a bouquet of sound
the sound of the tugboat
the wind in the trees
are not different
a dog barks
the bells ring.

19

Again winter
is only moons away
already sounds of night
gone south.

In this house
when wine is drunk
it's bound to be spilled.

The moon
is in the glass
when I salute it
my shadow and I
get this dance going.

After four glasses
who needs glasses?

Now to watch
the flies make love
while I stand outside
at the window.

20

Sparkles cross the bay for hours move
closer till they reach the dock
climb the wall
pierce the cathedral.
The boats have drifted the breeze risen
against the rocks dark blue light blue
shades of pink Grecian trees the ancient mariners
the flurry of wings on the rocks the seagulls
the albatross sky-weary

floating around the open boats
stripes of blue in the bay black
shadows of birds in the boudoir of sky
the sea with its phone poles.

With his head in the sky my son reaches
for Rousseau's discourse on inequality
and my Scotch
a sprig of soft hair swirls from his skull
from him I inhale the scent of his mother
see the children on the shore looking seaward.

The blackbirds have drifted
the sun once right before me lighting the sea
then forgotten
now bright to the west the horizon
with voyagers dropped below the trees
into the arms of grandmother night
her common sense how it warms us

while we row through centuries
while midnight crawls the shoreline
searching for sunrise.

Versions of Ryokan

I made this cane
from the horns of the wild hare.

I wove this robe
from particles of air.

I made these sandals
from the wool of the tortoise.

With my silent voice I sing these poems
so that everyone can hear.

★

The last of the geese heading south
in small flocks.

Autumn stretches out in front of me
leaves stripped from the mountains
by the frozen rain.

Faraway lit by sunset
a village is going to sleep.

★

Like clouds driven by strong winds
the business of this world transforms itself.

Fifty years now I have lived
one unbroken dream.

Late night showers fall quietly
on my woven shack
as I embrace my holy robes

and lean against the window
against the hollow
world.

          ★

On the road begging suddenly caught
in a storm I sought refuge
in the ruins of the village shrine.

To see me now you too would laugh
at my empty bowl and flask
and at how happy I am to find myself

in this abandoned shrine
overgrown with weeds.

          ★

Traveling around all these years covered
both court and country still

they are the same as ever.
I wish I could say the same for people!

Few live as well as those who've gone ahead.
Monk or layman everyone's out to destroy themselves.

Once a traveled path now
the highway of the spirit
lies beneath tall sharp grass.

                    ★

Walking all day to day's end begging for food
finally at my shack closing the door behind me
I build a fire with branches of dry leaves.

I read poems by the Cold Mountain hermit
while the wind swells in from the west
and drops its heavy rain.

My thatched roof weeps from the strain
but on the floor my legs stretched out before me
no doubts

nothing to worry about.

                    ★

Now as an old man
thoughts return to me
of my childhood.
I see myself alone
in a huge hall
reading a book,

the candle before me
replaced many times.

Back then
I knew not
the full length
of these winter nights.

       ★

With nothing but a robe and a bowl
I have covered so many miles.

Still on my journey
here I am sick
by a window
nursing myself with an incense burner
and the night.

The rain speaks to me
of ten years on the road.

       ★

Dragging my feet all day long
from village to village
not a thing in my bowl.

At sunset
still miles of mountainous road
before reaching my shack.

The wind parts my beard down the center,
my robes like thinning smoke,
my empty bowl deformed and discolored from use.

So it goes,
I can't complain nor spare my pains.
Cold and hungry
I go the path
of many a sage before me.

*

As a young boy I studied the arts and letters
and failed as a scholar.

As a young man I studied Zen
and failed to transmit the master's lamp.

Now I live in a shack made of grass
next to a shrine of the Shinto sect.

So, here I am, half shrine-keeper,
half priest.

*

Book after book making yourself
a warehouse of knowledge,

so much better to live
by one word of truth.
You ask: What is one word of truth?

Come, see your heart
as it really is!

*

For more than sixty years nothing
but a sickly priest.

Alone in my shack beside the temple
far way from the lights and smoke,

deep in the night the rains flood down
uprooting enormous rocks.

On the dark windowsill
candlelight

knocked around the room
by the wind.

*

Early on I put aside the ink stone and brush
and my heart chose the path of the ancients.
I wandered here and there with only a flask and bowl
for who knows how many years.

In a weed-ridden shack in the shade of a hill
I found repose.

Since then I've lived alone,
turning to the birds for music

to the white clouds crossing the sky
for companionship.

Streaming from beneath a massive rock
the clear spring water cleans the dust
from my robes.

Tall pines and oaks rise up to the heavens,
their leaves and branches
to warm me come winter.

With not a worry nor a care to disturb this peace
I live from day to day
till dawn appears no more.

The World of Difference

My Skull

Finally, dear skull, your appearance
delights me. For so long
I've known you were coming.
I saw it in my father and uncles,
I caught glimpses so soon
after puberty, that while a long
and thick mop of hair hung
below my shoulders there was
what seemed a constant breeze,
a headwind pushing the hair away
from my forehead, back, always back.
And with the sun blazing
through the thinning strands, you,
dear skull, blazed back.
It's gotten so that I wouldn't
recognize myself with too much hair,
nor do I think I would like who I saw:
that man, with a mouth of big teeth,
the face of a giant ant, and those eyes . . .
those eyes I've seen in photographs
when I was looking elsewhere—
the eyes of a blackbird, a scavenger
groveling and pecking, flying away
at the slightest noise. Silent cranium,
passing through it all: the odd jobs,
the inclement weather, the few hands
that have tousled my hair and rubbed
you, dear skull, the monk in me,
patiently making your way
to the clear sky
to bow.

Morning Meditation

Almost like sleep, but safer, since
there is no falling or rising.

To be there without being in any place;
without arriving, without plans to leave.

The trees don't know the season.
The pond doesn't know it's wet.

The sky rests on the grass and stones,
goes and remains.

The bells don't hear themselves.
The breeze doesn't make itself shiver.

The needle doesn't stick itself.
The cat doesn't preen before the mirror.

The tongue doesn't lick itself.
The rose doesn't swoon.

The eyes light on nothing
and are lost to themselves—

he doesn't know
he's not thinking.

Cricket

In the bush outside my window
you say the same thing over and over
with equal enthusiasm. Whatever it is,
I know it's the truth. No one could go on
so relentlessly if it wasn't.
What that truth is doesn't matter, finally,
because of your persistence.
I could hear you saying *cricket-cricket*
and translate it to *I am-I am!*
And just as easily I could hear the chirping
Fuck it-fuck it! and be equally moved
because I'm here by the window
where the stars are, where the half moon is.
Each morning, turning off the alarm,
stepping from the shower, drying myself,
tying my shoes, packing my bag . . .
When a car comes you become silent.
Too much noise shuts us both up.
Like you, I disappear all day.

Becoming a Buddha

Suddenly one morning I woke up and I had ass-belly!
   That's when a man's ass decides it's had enough, leaves
his bottom, moves to his front and settles on his belly.
   After forty or so years of reasonable comfort, the tired ass
leaves it up to the bones: "You do it, let him sit on you
   for a change." And the poor bones don't have a choice.
"Okay, ass," they say. "Be like that. You think you've
   had it bad! We're the last to go; we're the last to know
    the bastard's gone."

I sit here with arms folded over my newly relocated ass,
   and I finally understand the Buddha's big belly:
it takes this long to slow down and sit in the middle
   of the highway in rush hour, where traffic is a pin-drop
of sound, a solid brick of motion and there's no need,
   no desire to step on the gas and weave on through.
It takes this long to be reminded that soon enough
   it will be time to return this rented body to the dealer.

Now I have the Buddha's drooping ears to look forward to:
   old man ears, sacred elephant ears. Already my ears
are filling with hair. This is the forest where the Buddha sat.
   It happens, with enough time and in the right season,
that hearing hears itself.
   Then the earlobes become huge.

Cheap Shoes

White canvas slip-ons with a blue line
  like the trim on a yacht; such plain comfort
    for $5.99 that today someone said,
"Where are your shoes?" thinking they were my socks.
  But I feel luxurious, tropical, Panamanian,
    and so relaxed that there are palm trees, mangoes,
pink flamingoes every step I take in this flat
  mid-western American town. To match my mock
    elegance I wear my baggiest blue jeans,
four inches too large in the waist, my blousiest shirt
  unbuttoned half way, and a woman I hardly know
    stops me on the street and says, "You're so thin,
have you been ill?" But to me, this is the attire
  of a man with plenty of time to get from one place
    to another, time to sip an iced coffee, to browse
for hours the aisles of the bookstore and buy
  nothing, to saunter the baked white sidewalks,
    flat footed, tanned, not glossy with sweat. These
white shoes conjure up the old country: the piazzas,
  the chiming of the steeple bells, the rolled up
    sleeves of unshaven men playing bocce
in the cool shadow of the church, rough hands
  waving black cigars, juice glasses of red wine,
    the fig trees' black shade.
I jingle a pocketful of change to the tempo
  of some tune I've made up. But these cheap shoes
    have their own tune, quiet
as their soft rubber soles, they move
  in only one direction: to their own demise.
    The grid of the soles smoothes, the white

of the canvas dulls, the strength of the stitch collapses.
Months away, with a light snow falling,
I'll slip them on to take out the trash.

Snow

On our way out the door, my three-year-old son says,
"Dad, I have to poop."
After all the work of bundling him up,
"Go ahead," I say.
He sheds his parka, drops his snow pants,
and mounts the high white seat of the toilet.
I unbutton my overcoat, loosen my scarf,
let it hang from my neck, and wait.
Almost immediately he calls from the bathroom,
"Papa, check my bottom."
I lean over the small of his back as he bows
lost in the flurry of my overcoat and scarf.
I wipe his ass again. He hops off the toilet,
pulls up his pants. I flush and see shit
on the fringe of my scarf; disbelieving,
I hold it up to the light:
"There's shit on my scarf!"
He puts on his coat, mittens and hat.
I'm reminded of the young monk Ikkyu
wiping Kaso's shriveled ass with his bare hands,
washing his master's frail body, rinsing
the soiled sheets, wringing them out
day and night till the old man's death.
I think, too, of the stains on my father's bed,
the nurses drawing the curtains to clean him,
his sunken eyes, looking into mine, ashamed.
"It's all right, Dad," I say.
"It's not all right," he says.

My son tromps to the door, flings it open:
a blast of cold air rushes through the house.
I wash the fringe in the sink, tighten
my scarf and raise my collar.
He's making angels in the snow.

The Moments Noticed

Even with the keys in my hand
       as soon as I close the door
I wonder if I've locked myself out.

       Heat-waves on the black-top parking lot.
          One old grey Buick
     and a squirrel underneath eating French fries.

A swarm of blackbirds
       in the State House trees—
my boot heels sink into morning's mud.

       Tiny weed patch
          in the middle of the asphalt parking lot—
     one cricket's island.

Opening the door, the curtains
       reach out and greet me
like a pair of angels.

       Rice, beans, pickles—
          big sink,
     one dish.

The TV on, the sound off—
       a face to look at
when I look up.

One long hair in the sink—
a G clef
gone grey.

Books lined up beside the bed—
tonight
the titles are enough.

Liturgy

—for Scott

Removing myself
    from a busy street
        to a doorway,
or from an open field
        to heavy limbs overhead—
           standing still and not
wanting it to stop, wanting instead
        to remain inside
           the white hum
of the downpour.

In the small space
    of a stranger's doorway,
        or among the dry needles
beneath the pine boughs,
    sometimes under a stone bridge
        or on the stoop of a creaking porch;
sometimes just sitting by an open window,
    or pausing at the front door
        before leaving, I submit
to this prayer,
    the chapel:
        the rain.

Heaven Now or Never

Above me
    a leaf
of warm dust
    falling
from the heat vent
    plays a Hendrix solo
plucking, pulling and
    bending the air
till it bows, rocks
    then rests
on the floor.

    Cigarette smoke
    curling from an ashtray
    in Paris
    twenty-five years before
    makes my tired
    eyes tear.

A man in my twenties
    walks all night,
so many nights too late
    for the last subway.
He raises his collar
    against the cold
and clutches his throat.
    Dead leaves shuffle
like a brush on a high hat,
    every step a crisp snap,

every footfall a drum kick.
        Twenty years until
he gets here.

        Wind chimes
        clang the green wood
        of a porch among trees
        where a bird the size,
        shape and color
        of a pine cone
        suddenly bursts
        into flight, a blur.

Homage to Ryokan

I drink my fill.

     The clouds grip their purple,
     the mountains let go their thunder.

I sit and drink my fill.

     How much I long to see
     through the man
     who sees through the moment.

I sit.

Homage to Issa

It rains.
       So it rains.

I wait beneath a tree
       and the tree is just an Ash.

Cicadas and crickets?
       They are only cicadas and crickets.

The river is just a river,
       night is simply dark,
              the stars are simply stars.

Granted, sometimes the leaves seem more
       than leaves—the heron shriek,
           the owl hoot—

       but the moon is just the moon.

A bonfire burns in the valley, the snow falls
       and neither
           are heaven or hell.

My bed is a bed,
       not a grave.

My hands are just hands,
       not wings.

My shoes are shoes
and I'm not Achilles.

Issa says: "Frog and I, eyeball to eyeball."
That's good enough for me.

Homage to My Father

My father said:
>   Fuck Father Farrell,
>>   what does *he* know, that old bastard!

Study all the religions. Learn Italian.
>   See Venezia, Firenze, talk
>>   to all kinds of people

and never, never think you know more
>   than someone else! Unless,
>>   unless they're full of shit.

And if they are, tell them;
>   and if they still don't get it, fuck it,
>>   there's nothing you can do about it.

Learn how to bake bread.
>   If you can make pasta and bake bread
>>   you can always feed your family,

you can always get a job.
>   Keep your house clean
>>   and don't worry what anyone else does.

Cut your grass,
>   prune your fruit trees
>>   or they'll die on you.

Don't drink too much
    but don't always be sober—
        it makes you nervous.

A couple glasses of wine,
    some anisette now and then,
        a cigar never hurt nobody.

Nervous people always got an ache here,
    an ache there, they get sick,
        they die—

Look at Father Farrell:
    he'll be dead in a year.
        Fuck him!

Balzac and the Buddha

I haven't read much Balzac
    but I like to say his name.

It's the name I give to the hostess
    while waiting in line for a seat.

It delights me to hear over the intercom:
    "Balzac, party of three."

When I was in the Buddhist monastery
    the Master would shout, "Katz!"

and I would reply, "Balzac!"
    He would hit me with his withered stick.

I once knew a dyslexic accountant;
    he was often black and blue

and looking for work.
    When he went to the Buddhist monastery

and the Master shouted, "Katz!"
    he punched the Master,

and the Master said, "Balzac."
    The cook, overhearing this encounter,

merely muttered, "Rabelais."
    That's why he's the cook;

he knows where his belly is.
          When I say the word "Buddha,"

my two-year-old son shoots his finger
          straight into the air.

I tell him that someday Balzac
          will cut that finger off.

He grins, lifts his bottle
          and says, "Juice!"

Before enlightenment there is, it is said,
          chopping wood and carrying water.

After enlightenment there is, it is said,
          chopping wood and carrying water.

Somewhere in between
          is the ferry.

Balzac.

The Vulture

We hate the vulture because he preys upon the dead.
  We have this thing about the dead: flowers
which live and die, we give to the dead;
  a casket to preserve the body we give to the dead;
someone makes money, people feel better;
  a headstone, a gardener we give to the dead.
We don't like the idea of eating the defeated.
  We loathe the idea of our bones picked clean
bleached white and brittle by the sun.

But in the Himalayas, the vultures are the reincarnations
  of Buddhists monks. The people revere the vulture
because it does not kill in order to survive.
  The eyes of the vulture and the eyes of the monk
sitting on top of a mountain for thirty years and more
  are no different—they settle on the complete stillness
of the shrubs and flowers, the sand and snow,
  the fields where the yaks feed, the sheep graze.

The wings of the vulture are as strong as an eagle's.
  But while the eagle scopes out its prey, spies
the rabbit eating clover, circles, then plummets
  filled with ambition and determination, the vulture
practices patience, lifted by the heat waves,
  by the shifting winds—stillness will come;
stillness always comes. We hate the vulture.

We bury the bones and pick our memories clean.
   With the body buried we can re-create the body
in whatever image, whatever likeness we want.
   We make everything right, as it should've been,
with flowers, with candles, with a fine coffin
   that neither time nor nature can erode.
We think we have had the last say. The dead
   bury the dead. But the vulture—like the monk,
like the gravedigger—does not discriminate.
   It's nothing personal.

You Can Stay, You Can Go

Here among pack dogs
        and pine trees, it's possible
to become rock and banyon,
        bark and patter of coyote.

You can stay, you can go.

Knee-cracking zazen,
        four months of mountain summer,
snow, ice, a flood of sunlight
        and mud.

You can stay, you can go.

The clouds below the mountain
        are a walkway to LA—
a bowl of steel wool.

You can stay, you can go.

Monk foot: when the dried
        soles look like street maps
cut by a razor.

You can stay, you can go.

Monk dick: pissing
        in a bucket of stars
at three in the morning.

You can stay, you can go.

Every asshole
      is your master.
Can you eat bitter?

You can stay, you can go.

Some pass through the needle,
      some hear the pebble hit bamboo,
some lift a flower and grin,
      some lift a glass and laugh.

You can stay, you can go.

When everyone's a Thou,
      thus are thee—to bow
means to bend the body.

You can stay, you can go.

The Ones Who Stay

Young Shakyamuni would've been a deadbeat dad
if he hadn't come from a rich family—wife and son
provided for within the walls, without the trash,

while he was out sitting under a tree in the forest
being fed a berry at a time by passing birds
six years or so; then came the goat cheese.

The ones who stay may not know the Bodhi tree,
but they learn the alchemy of credit, the strategies
of insurance policies, unemployment, accidental death.

If only he could sit in the treetop
outside his window and prune the dead
branches from last spring's winter storm

he might fly, he might pass through rocks
and stone walls, be five places at once,
comfortable and saintly in each.

Pack the lunch, fold the laundry,
help with the homework, read aloud
the veins of the chipped ceiling, sleep.

The morning monk with the wake-up bell
is older by centuries
than old Shakyamuni himself.

Home on Business

for Marly

Alone for the night at home with my wife
        away on business. It doesn't get any better
            than this: feed the dog, crank the tunes,
make a chicken sandwich and open a beer.
        Watch the news; leave the dishes for later.
            I smoke a cigar in the sunroom, catch
the sun setting, the pine shadows trembling,
        and have another Schlitz, a shot of Chivas,
            stroll from Monk to Steven Reich, from
Bartok to Ahmad Jamal, Randy Weston,
        Leon Parker, Sun Ra and late Coltrane
            in Tokyo, all because I want to weep
and there's no one here to leave the house
        in a huff or go crazy. I pace and brood,
            and turn the lights on in every room, busy,
looking with the eyes of a public official,
        for solid evidence, for clues of some kind.
            What is this? Who belongs to this stuff?
It's not so much a matter of what I do
        with these vacant, unscheduled hours,
            what matters now is doing it alone—back
to the body I was born with, this coffin
        that will find its way to a furnace; flame
            to dull ash, bone cinders to grey soil,
white smoke turned to blue weather.
        Without you: the necessary sweat lodge,
            the temple cave, the cathedral at Chartres,

the Ryokan hut after the thief forgot to take the moon
along with the rest of his things.
Our roof, these walls, this floor: a shack,
a cardboard box, a shrub, a palace, a cave,
a Gethsemane, this grove of evergreens:
wind comes, rain comes, and I stand here
in the midst of it, dry and wrapped in these pliant boughs,
falling with the rain all night, alone and grateful
that this, my love, is our home.

The Hands

At night, the hands
        come to the face
and push it together again.

The hands know the terrain,
        have always known
how day disfigures the face.

The fingers push the layers,
        rub and spread the skin around,
find their place

closest to the skull.
        Skin and bones of my spirit,
crawl space, temple, cave,

waiting room and cathedral
        for many other spirits, at night
the hands come to the face

and push it together again.

        ★

It's the cold
        that puts one hand
inside the other,
        like prayer. The trains go by,

the cold stays.
It's the cold
            that puts one hand
inside the other,
            as in waiting
for a train, as in waiting,
            waiting,
one hand
            for the other.

                    *

The cold pushes
            the blood aside
                        howls
through veins
            to heart, from heart
                        throughout
the limbs.
            Hands and feet
                        frantic for heat;
old hands reaching
            from the dark
                        to the flames.

Tokudo Shiki

In the eyes of a squirrel
    and the flash of its tail.
In a bone white tree trunk
    and the wind that's worn it away.
In the brush of the fly's wings
      sweeping the dust from his ears.
           Seido makes his home.

In the teats of an old street bitch
     scraping the sidewalk.
In the blue jay collecting rent
     with its sharecropper song.
In the mosquito concerto
    taking his blood for a ride.

In the trees turning in a huff
    and slamming their doors.
In the outstretched wings of a hawk—
    the black wink of a blue eye.
In the shadow he feeds to the rocks
    one footstep at a time.

In the thick sap of a pinecone
    slapping his black sleeve as he passes.
In the moon bright trunks and rocks
    guiding him to his door.
In the mouse he catches with light,
    opening the cupboard, hungry.
         Seido makes his home.

THIS RENTED BODY

A Drop in the Temperature

Grey sky and earth
        getting hard. Squirrels
burrowing through the piles
        of brown and blackened
leaves. Blue jays crying
        like the rusted pulley
of the clothesline
        as my mother reels in
the damp clothes
        before it snows.

An iron grey branch
        claws at the roof
while winds tumble
        down from the north. My jaw
hangs slack.
        The same at forty-seven as I was
before I could count:
        gazing at the stiff lawn,
listening
        to the blue jays, a little boy
in mittens, flannel-lined
        pants, a jacket too big
with a hood that looks
        forward even though
I turn my head.
        The neighborhood
is silent
        the way someone

who knows something
        doesn't say.

My mother asks me
        to help her sort
and fold the laundry,
        but I don't want to.
I want to stay outside.
        I don't need to be
a soldier, a cowboy
        or a knight in armor.
I pick up a branch
        that's neither a gun
nor a sword. Now,
        and so many times
since then, my eyes settle
        on a twig, a stone,
a swatch of grass and I can't
        look away. My mother
goes inside and slams
        the warped door shut.

Federal Hill, RI

They yelled under the grape vines
        whatever they said;
in the evening, in the midst of fig trees,
        tomato plants, lettuce,
string beans, cucumbers,
        spinach, chicory,
the yellow rose bushes surrounding
        the blue Madonna,
geraniums, chrysanthemums.
        Grandpa
rocking far back in his iron chair
        smoking fat black cigars,
drinking black red wine pressed
        and stored in the damp dirt cellar.
The picnic table covered with plates
        of biscotti, rumballs,
spinach pie, doughboys, a wooden
        bowl of grapes
green and bitter, blemished
        peaches, hard green apples,
Mangia! Mangia! Food I never
        had at home—cakes
made with anisette, with brandy,
        ripe figs right from the tree . . .
the smoke from cigars
        and cigarettes burned
my eyes, made me cough and dream
        all night: *carpaccio, va bene,*

prosciutto e fichi, benissimo, eco—
    tossing and wriggling as if
tied to a beam in the dank cellar,
    I'd sit up in bed,
bolted to the dark,
    while my father's snoring
prowled throughout the house.

The Things They Keep

The ugly, and less ugly paintings;
       bone-dry books held for thirty, forty years.
            Not the favorite sweaters, threadbare,
stretched; most comfortable shoes, shirts;
       no one wants the slippers and robe,
            the winter hat, the parched leather gloves.
The eyeglasses are worthless, the razor
       and toothbrush. The favorite towel, good
            for washing the car, for drying the lawn-
chairs after a sunshower. Give away
       the pants and suits, throw out the socks,
            the underwear, the neckties, the hand-
kerchiefs, the sweat-weathered wallets kept
       in the top drawer with the dead watches,
            the cufflinks, the tie clips, tie tacks.

            Who wants the ball of string, the tool box?

What once was held knew its worth
       by the hands that held it. Now the black
            umbrella sticks out of the trash, a wilted
stalk. The suitcase that crossed continents
       waits on the sidewalk for the dump truck.
            As they go, their things go too: who,
a week later, a month, a year, thinks
       long about the dead? A pain now and then
            like an old injury before the rain falls—

sudden, brief, a sharp reminder. Then
the news comes: It's time to put your things
in order. Beyond a generation or two,
nothing you can hold in your hands will last.
All that was said, all that was done—
this alone they keep.

Nola's Banana Nut Bread

Four inches of windblown powder
        on a six inch ice-packed base.

I run and slide, run
        and slide up the street

in the wiry shadows of creaking trees,
        seven blocks skating

streetlight to streetlight
        with a loaf of Nola's

banana nut bread tucked
        under my arm. The falling

snow looks like minnows
        swimming the white light

of the elms. I'd rather be
        skating the frozen

snowy canals of Amsterdam
        on my way

to a coffeeshop
        off Prinsengracht, a place

where I don't expect to understand
        the language, where

I know I won't run into my ex-wife
    and her boyfriend,

a place where I can sip
    rich coffee, enjoy a chunk

of dark chocolate, smoke
    and watch the snow

pile up in the corners
    of the windowsill.

Long icicles hang from the rusted
    fire escape above

the back door to my building.
    The ivy is a mess

of brown string. The cars
    parked in the lot

of the Senior Citizens' Home
    haven't moved for days, thick

with ice and snow. My home
    is as I left it: Sunday paper

spread on Wednesday's floor,
    cups, empty beer cans,

sweaters draped on chairbacks.
    My coat slumps

keeled over on the couch
        asleep. My wet boots

leave puddles and sand
        on the kitchen floor

as I cut a half dozen thin slices
        of bread and slide them

into the oven. This is not
        a barge, ice-locked

in the city of a thousand bridges,
        this is a small apartment

in Lincoln, Nebraska: outside
        only the flashing yellow lights

of the sand truck and plow.
        Thank you, Nola.

It's too late to phone my son
        sound asleep on the far side

of town; it's too soon
        to fall in love, too expensive

to go out for a few drinks,
        too early to go to bed and

not sleep. It's just right
        for hot home-made bread.

Bicycle

Locked to the fence, the chain links
overgrown with ivy, the handle bars,
seat, front fork, spokes, tires all
in a snare of green leaves and blue buds.
Tires soft, almost flat. Rust forming
where the frame's chipped and scarred.
Even the lock, caked with orange, seems
impossible to undo. Each day as I pass you
locked in the grip of the dense vines,
I miss the banking and turning, following
the wind one moment, fighting it the next,
keeping an eye on the clouds, planning
where to lock you in case of rain.
The breeze lifts the morning glories
from your blue metallic frame. Small
consolation, this retirement
among the sprawling, leafy vines
and abundant blossoms. You've become
a trellis: no longer a moving thing,
but a thing moved upon.

Sheer Hunger

Some asshole, (I assume
he was an asshole),
threw half a loaf of bread
in the middle of a busy street.
A gang of blackbirds slammed
onto the burning asphalt
jabbing and clawing each other,
talons and beaks stabbing
at the bread.

I drove up at 40 mph
and all at once they exploded
into the air like gushing oil;
all the birds, that is, but one.

This one, so determined
for bread, so set on her path,
whether courageous or plain
stupid, made me swerve
at the very last minute
and swerve again
back to my own side
of the shimmering street.

When I glanced
in the rearview mirror,
that bird hadn't budged.
There she pecked,
all alone, a brick of bread
twice her size.

A Wall of Books

Dim and bright brick tight
    against brick—the books
        that line the walls

have themselves become
    wall. Up close
        the dull bindings,

their colors, drained
    by sweat, are the cracks
        in the mortar

where suddenly day appears:
    the dirt street
        where an ox roams

into the thicket
    and the oxherder
        draws him back.

A bird flaps for a clawhold
    on a sick man's
        windowsill.

Trees leap across meadows
    and Busby Berkeleyites kick
        heel-toe through town.

White clouds pile up
        on jagged peaks. Children
                toss handfuls of grass

in each others' face and laugh.
        A cuckoo stuttering
                most tentatively.

Horseflies in a house
        surrounded
                by dung—this

is why their spines have bled.
        When flocks swing by
                wheeling and turning

I see them. When dawn's blossoms
        open their rosy petals
                and a woman puts on her lipstick,

I see them. When the temple bells grieve
        and the night monkeys chatter
        and the cicadas

rattle themselves to death, I hear them.
        When an old friend says,
                Why not drink

one more glass of wine.
Beyond Yang Pass
there are only strangers.

I don't hesitate.

Pistachio Nuts

There are those with mouths
    wide open, ready
        to be taken.

Those with a sideways grin
    who require some
        prodding.

But every one will be consumed
    sooner or later, even those
        clamped shut,

shell and all popped
    into the mouth
        to savor the salt,

to soften the shell,
    to bite gently
        to the cracking point

where it's tooth
    or pistachio—suddenly
        soft, the break,

the taste!
    The time it took
        never happened.

Green Beans

The joy
    comes not from planting
        but from having
the sense
    to buy five cans for a dollar
        this week, four
for a dollar last week
    and the week before that—
        water, low salt, no fat
a delicacy
    when cold and smothered
        with vinegar and tarragon.
I have known what it's like
    to have Cheerios in ginger ale,
        tomato paste soup,
my last few cigarettes
    carefully lined up
        on the cluttered desk.
The tarragon
    makes all the difference
        in the late night news.
I know I'm being good
    to myself despite
        the riots,
shattered windows,
    anthrax mail,
        and smart bombs.
The half bright moon
    and a light stream of traffic.
        The taste of malt,

spice oil in the vinegar,
      a dash of pepper,
           a sprinkle of salt—
of course,
      more than just a hint
         of garlic.

Walking in Winter

for Tim Skeen

Midwestern wind is sneaky.
        It leans against your back
with a gentle nudge going south,
        then it strips your face to tears
tromping north towards home.

Like everything else that throws on clothes
        and heads out the door,
there's a price to pay for walking away.
        Another price to pay for walking home.
And walk we did: collars raised,
        gloved hands and covered heads
for the sake of putting one foot in front
        of the other, a sign: we're not done yet.

We covered miles—frigid twigs, frozen
        bird baths, frosted leaves, icicles
three feet long dripping from the 4th floor
        of the Haymarket seed factory
"could kill somebody" you said.

We'd already seen what cancer
        and a policeman's bullet
could do to a family, a walk
        against a hammering wind
was a history exam we already
        knew all the answers to.

But did we know, could we possibly
        know how many pairs of shoes would pass
between us and the pavement?
        Worn out soles stacked in our closets,
how we refuse to throw the lifeless
        fish back into the sea.

And how many still? Each day
        when I walk, I say to myself
what I've always said.
        Every man needs a brother,
every walk deserves another.

Cockroach

In a dusty corner near the couch
    you lie
legs up, for weeks out of reach
    of the vacuum cleaner.
Like the wing with leg and talon
    still attached
flattened in the gutter
    on 9th St., more
clumps of feathers
    scattered
around the park, the squirrel
    in the middle
of D St.—here
    in a pile of dust
by the wall, your black
    brittle shell
is just one more place
    to enter, a small
shrine
    to kneel down in
and say a prayer.

In death, you are
    like the stone temples
in the Dutch farmland,
    a single statue
and room enough
    for one person

to escape the rain and wind
        and kneel.
My eyes rest on you
        as the wine-soaked
conversation drifts away.
        It's good to leave
the table through you
        and be off
to where the day's gossip
        doesn't reach,
where there are no
        obligations to confess
sins or goals
        to anyone, including
myself. Through you
        whatever we were
talking about becomes
        a moment
of crows
        in the sugarbeet fields
and wild sunflowers
        twelve feet tall.

Jerusalem Slim

Tall, paunched,
      a bright beam
of baldness
      on the back of his skull;
his beard is fat
      like a steel-wool sheep.
His forehead sparks
      with sweat.
Walk faster
      when the leaves fall
and the ground freezes,
      he says. Slow down
when the sidewalk
      sizzles, wear a hat—
it keeps you cool.
      Leaving and
arriving, what does it matter?
      One foot after another
makes its own sense.
      Love your feet,
care for them as you would
      the small, delicate
feet of a child. Soak them,
      rub them, let them
feel the air. No matter
      how thin the sleeves
of your coat, warm shoes
      will keep you warm

all winter. Snow flurries,
        sun showers . . . leave
the flowers intact. Love
        them, love your feet
and the rest
        will take care of itself.

Thirteen Keys

An "endless ring" I was taught
by the jeweler and watchmaker—
a double circle in steel, silver, gold.

At the end of the day
I see the darkened circle
on my index finger from
twirling my key ring of
thirteen keys like a cowboy
his pistol into the holster.
It's only natural, unlocking
one door after another,
to want to celebrate by
rattling the keys a few
times just for the tune
of it. Dark is the circle
where I twirl the ring
and worn is the skin
so much that it shines.

Burano, Italy

Whoever comes and goes
    must come and go by boat;
        the only way to Burano

has always been a matter of sea,
    a matter of moon. Bright yellow,
        purple, pink, blue homes

reflected in canal water
    red, orange, white ripples so
        painted because once upon a time

when the sailors still came home
    from sea it was easier for sea-legs
        to stagger from ship to tavern,

from tavern to home's front door.
    There are no sailors anymore.
        And only the old ladies still make lace—

eyes worn out, sunk in chiseled faces; arthritic hands
    ply only a few hours each day while the young tell
        their grandmothers' stories to tourists.

Windows wide open the lace curtains shuffle.
    Doors wide open the old ladies mumble
        one to another, or to no one.

There are tablecloths, curtains, shawls behind glass
that will never be for sale—works of art
the family will never part with:

to see but neither touch nor buy, so
the granddaughter tell us:
Someday this will all be over; no one,

none of the young girls has the time or
the desire to learn lace making anymore.
Just look at them! Look at them.

You see what I mean?
Machines, machines can do it better for less;
you know what I mean?

The sound of shallow water laps the hulls
of the brightly painted boats; the gruff
cacophony of vendors in the marketplace

rouses the appetite; a table outside,
an umbrella to block the sun, the smell
of fresh bread and flowers, a cold beer.

A toothless grin in a black lace shawl
smiles at me: I am old.
A lacemaker in the shadows.

Elegy for a Book of Poems

for "Kentucky Swami"

*You're right, the mill never missed
your paycheck. Thirty years
and never a mistake.
You're a simple man, as you say.*
—Tim Skeen

Laid to rest: the years in hours; daily
        a long walk
to a blank page and bowing
        at his desk like a monk
as words appear
        and disappear into the union line,
the steel mill, the strut
        of an MP in a country not his.
It's over.

The hours
        he chiseled into moments
are sealed in poems like dreams,
        like dreams the blue jay,
the cat's tail, the strangers
        playing baseball,
the raccoon stiff
        on its side by the highway.
His daughter
        will become her mother
and him,
        and be herself.

The book has made it so.
     And now what's said about the swami
is what's said about the dead.
     The Greeks called it "kleos."
In this way
     they rivaled the gods.

Till Death Do Us Part

for Marly

One funeral after another
      creates an odor that
lingers in the nostrils,
      a perfume
that conjures up
      an unforgiving silence
that makes even the breath
      stop until a long sigh
starts it up again.
      "I love you" means
I love myself too much
      to do nothing, too much not
to make myself part
      of the larger picture that
seats me beside her
      at the dining room table,
that places me
      before a sink full of dishes,
that has me checking
      the refrigerator and cupboards
while making the grocery list,
      that puts me on my knees
pulling weeds from the garden,
      standing in a daze
watering the lawn. We
      glance at one another
in the mirror: me, brushing
      my teeth; she, soaking

her contact lenses. Time
       has not stopped for this
belly of mine nor
       for the grey and white strands
that streak her long brown hair.
       The daily routines have slowed
the passage of years not
       by weeks or months but by
knowing what wine to buy
       for dinner, what dessert
we both enjoy, what movies
       we want to rent, what vitamins
we need, what route is best
       for a slow walk after dinner;
by knowing, night after night
       on what side of the bed
to lie—to be so close
       to someone that her scent
overpowers the candles,
       the incense and flowers
on the altar. And sleep,
       when it comes,
comes easily,
       and is deep.

The Genius

It's as though
his head

were cut off
but his will

to live
made a face

of his neck;
so it looks

like he has
no neck,

when really
he has no head.

Old Monks Drinking

Bassui Roshi didn't fool around: *One who hands a glass*
of wine to another encouraging him to drink it will be born
for 500 lifetimes without hands. How many hundreds more
to he who hands the glass to himself?

At Kogaku-An he built a shrine to Basshushin: Lord
of the eternal hangover. As a brother monk once said:
"Sure, I'm a monk, but I never said I was a good one!"

He filled my teacup with Courvoisier and we stepped
outside behind the cabin for a cigar. All day zazen since
3:00 a.m.—chanting, working, sitting, sanzen with Roshi.

Every moment, including this one, a koan. We didn't speak.
We stood, sipped brandy from one hand and drew tobacco
from the other. Stared, mainly, at the black sky bright with

stars, satellites, passenger planes leaving LAX. So many
nights over twenty years standing in that spot—coyotes, scorpions,
pack dogs, bears, rattlesnakes, the outhouse breeze—pondering

the final destination of those planes. Where is your home?
The bell rings: More zazen! Standing on the mountain looking
into the jeweled valley with the burn of cognac and the bite

of tobacco on the tongue, blowing smoke. Two old monks.
In silence we finished; in silence went to our bunks
and once again put the skeleton down.

> *May I be born without hands for 500 lifetimes, for a*
> *thousand more lifetimes, if to be without hands means to*
> *need nothing yet give myself always to what's needed.*

My Mother Laughs from Heaven

So. Everyone you pass
      on the street has been your
            mother, father, sister or brother

at least once. But not
      the animals. No, son, as wicked as
            you are you've never

been a bird or a dog, a frog
      or a snake. But, if you can
            think of a time before

time and build a nest there, then
      you can become a bird
            if you really want to.

Just listen. Trees are made of bone.
      The sky is your home.
            That bullfrog is your father.

Homage to Kanzan

Again winter is only moons away.
      Already sounds of night gone south.

In this house, when wine is drunk
      it's bound to be spilled.

The moon is in the glass. When I lift it,
      my shadow and I get this dance going.

After three or four glasses,
      who needs glasses?

Diamond Cutter

Listen: a nightingale strains her voice, serenading the snow.
Look: a tortoise wearing a sword climbs the lampstand.
                                          —Hakuin

The doctor came to take his pulse and said
"Everything seems just fine." Winter, 1768.

In three days I'll be dead. Some doctor you are!

Ice on the branches, limbs bowed low,
the bald moonlight; the snowy wind,
the clatter and squeak of bamboo.

He woke and gave a shout
then turned on his side and died,
December 11th. Hakuin Ekaku.

If you want the great tranquility,
prepare
to sweat white beads.

His last words—ashes the color of coral,
the scent of jasmine; just before going
he took up the brush and wrote:

Sitting still in the midst of this flaming world
is a billion times better than sitting still in quiet.

One kanji—*In the midst!*

By noon the ice had melted,
the branches stood tall again.

Losing My Voice

You know when the lid slams shut?
You know when the stone ball drops
from the brain down through the body
to the soles of the feet? You know
the thud it makes? You know how
the throat feels tight and the stomach
swells, and the eyes ache even though
it's dark out? You know how your foot
taps without you and you crave things
that can kill you? Always it's 3 a.m.
no matter what time of day, and
you keep telling yourself, it's okay,
it's okay. You know how one morning
you realize you're not getting old,
you already are? And for that one
brief moment there's no joy
in the gingko tree, no red
in the Japanese maple,
and your walking stick is turning
into a hand-worn cane. You know
how you don't care how you look
at the supermarket? You don't care
if the car's dirty? Bottles, cans, bones:
it's all trash anyway. You know
when you're broke and the credit card
companies tack late fees on your bill?
What can you say? So many voices
already and so few matter, why listen

to my own? Why should my magnolias
matter, because they're mine? Why
should midnight with January snow
under the blue-white pine trees matter?
Because I see it? Or because it is seen
and has always been seen by the Greek
soldier, the Chinese hermit, the Italian
shepherd, the camel jockey, the piper fitter,
the stone cutter, the foundry worker,
the electrician, the shoe salesman—all
of them on their way somewhere, even
the milkman with his hobby: a prize pig.
The breakfast special that everyone
can afford: how does it come to matter
so much? And then not at all?
When I had a voice I listened to it
like a total stranger. He kept me up
nights, too many nights perhaps, but
he took me out to interesting places.
We lived in France, Holland, England;
we lived as mountain monks above
the clouds in California. We shoveled
summer snow, went days without sleep.
We discussed life from the point of view
of the dead, and death from the point of view
of the insatiable, the reckless, the joyous.
How does it happen that silence
is the better voice? The spruce trees make

no sound, nor does the blue jay when it
sings to itself. Where are the odes to shoes
and socks, fish and eggplant, thread,
hands, tomatoes, atoms, rocks, artichokes,
bocce and old wine fresh beneath the cork?
They're here, all right, in the trashcan
where the head bows and these old
shoulders push up hard against the tin lid
and nothing happens
again.

THE SKELETON OF THE CROW
Homage to Ikkyu

The Skeleton of The Crow

Words
            fail.
Mind
            fails.

Words
on the page,

of wind
in the trees—

who hears it?

Used books
are good buys.

          ★

Wind chimes
nudged

prodded

poked by hours
of sun

the quiet   .
hours of moon.

If you must
believe,

believe
in the one

facing you
now.

Squint
and see—

fuck flattery!

★

With so many
words

why waste time
on just a few?

Use them all
until you choke.

We walk
but never see

the skeleton—
the breath,
blood and bones

that deliver
the squirrels

to the porch.

*

Stuck nowhere
the wind

just visits
place to place,

never forgets
its job for long.

Not two, not one,
not many—

this monk is guilty

of hanging from a branch
by his teeth.

Not asking how,
not asking why—

mountain rockhopper
when it lands

disappears
in the shimmering scree.

Grass,

sky,   rain,

wind,   mountain,   valley,

steel,   glass,   brick—

Not two, not one.
Not many.

What could be worse
than nature?

Spring comes

but not till the wind
has frozen the earth.

★

What's more perfect
than nature?

Not a tree nor brick
will mourn you.

★

The dead sing
under the grass.

Press your ear
to the tombstone

listen to the songs
you'll sing.

Stepping into heaven,
stepping into hell.

Big deal! *No One*
is the one

who walks away
from both.

★

Hit me once
I show you forgiveness.

Hit me twice
I show you compassion.

Hit me again, my wisdom
will kick your ass!

★

Sometimes
I'm just a storm

pouring myself
onto everything—

then the mosquitoes
rule the porch.

Someone said, "At birth
you cry and others laugh;

at death others cry
and you laugh."

How are you born?

Coffee, cream, one sugar.

⋆

Mother used to feed the birds,

pour boiling water
on the frozen birdbath—

a dimpled woman, fat—
day old bread in her hands.

⋆

Like sitting in boiling water
long hours legs crossed on the cushion—

fire, water, wind—the earth
turns and my bony ass burns.

Grey-haired lust:
ignorance grass.

One beautiful woman
after another

doing her errands
enters my sleep.

      ★

This body wants
to listen and touch,

fuck, and forget
about dying for a change.

Scotch on the rocks and *Oh!*
my Darlin' Clementine!

      ★

Most of my life
already lived—

what's left?

How many times
must I tell myself?

Not two, not one.
Not many.

Getting tired
is easy.

Getting exhausted
is hard work.

Great faith
in something

out of this world.

*

Like cows, horses—
fuck poetry!

A life standing
and grazing—

barbecue
and glue.

*

Lightning splits
the tree in half—

alive in both worlds
the earthworms

make the soil
moist and rich.

All night, cicadas and crickets.

I brush my teeth
wash my face.

Put the skeleton down,
let the skeleton dream.

★

I sit zazen
like a hawk

spreading its wings,
hungry—

eyes and limbs
knowing

where the food
is.

★

That she
could even love me—

her sweet
wrinkled face

when we awaken.

The totality
of reality—

shit and piss.

What is sweet
to the tongue

dissolves.

Who is
the One

who wants
a taste?

*

Being and non-being
embrace and separate—

without thinking
I swat the mosquito on my head.

Seeing, I wipe our blood
on my sleeve.

Every moment

when not thinking

I breathe

this wrinkled skin

that shivers

with what's invisible.

*

Is there a god or isn't there?
Is there a me or isn't there?

Answer one
you answer both.

In the meantime,
black tea while it rains.

These books on my shelf
like lovers I remember

who changed my life
for better, for worse.

*

My youth is gone, still
I raise the ax high

let it drop on its own
to split log after log

no matter how many times
I miss and groan

again.

*

My house—ashes, empty bottles,
not from a day but from many—

all I've loved and love:
stacked, tossed, sacked.

Before bed I long
to embrace

my mother
my father

so long in their graves—

brush my teeth,
piss goodnight.

★

Night and day
the invisible world

serenades earth
from soil to sea to sky.

This open window
without footsteps.

★

Under the footsteps
of a ten-ton fly

who sips the sweat
from my shiny skull.

"I'm just eating my ice cream."
My wife looks at me

like a child
sweet Jesus

would be proud of.

★

The gates of heaven,
the gates of hell,

kick them open hard
and arrive exactly

where *home sweet home*
has always been.

★

Tonight the sun
a bright ripe plum

robbed me of
old age and memories—

come sunset
the same old me.

Once you visit no-man's-land
it's clear—

In the beginning was the Word.

If that doesn't make you laugh,
nothing will.

★

A cart without wheels
a trough for pigs—

so easy to get sick,
tired of dragging

this bone-sack sagging
one sneeze to the next.

★

The day begins,
the day ends

but not really.

So many words,
so many dreams—

just to see, smiling
in the mirror,

the eyes of a crow.

Who among us is not
both sinner and saint?

The air is full of stones—
blind fools!

Who among us has neither
mother nor father?

*

Before sunrise
I step onto my porch

into a spider's web—

not two, not one.
Not many.

*

My flesh and bones
have yet to realize

they're already dead—

each morning
morning wood.

Flies comes out
of nowhere.

Like ants, worms
and mosquitoes

I also come from nowhere
Not two, not one. Not many.

⋆

I never claim to have
the perfect vision.

I see only what I see
with great doubt

as to who is seeing
and what is seen.

⋆

You cannot share,
as much as you want to,

that moment
when sunrise

steals your eyes
and you have nothing

to say for yourself.

I breathe in and out
until I breathe no more.

Bodhidharma faced the wall—
none of what he saw was true.

⋆

Drunk, sober,
nothing lasts forever—

Thus come, thus go!
So goes the Old Crow.

Where does the old
crow

go?

⋆

Shaving my head
again and again

the raw skin of my skull
glows like a baby's butt—

no longer a baby, but . . .
still I rise and glow.

Does the universe shine
all the way up your asshole?

If there's no Buddha
when wiping your ass

there's no Buddha.

★

The moon is one thing,
rice wine quite another.

Compassion, empathy,
forgiveness is rice wine.

Sitting down with just the moon
is irresponsible.

★

I can shed tears
when I talk to my son—

his music, like mine—

we both make sound
our own way.

As an altar boy in the Catholic Church I prayed—
Forgive me father, for I have sinned.

Fifty years old now, a Zen monk, I chant—
Infinite are all beings, I vow to save them.

*

Memories flee—no more the taste
I once thought them to be—

sweat salty—loving those

I thought I would love
and love and love forever.

*

When the Master dies,
What then? What then?

While the Master lives,
What now? What now?

When will these monks
ever learn to just smile?

Still

      move

breath

      breeze

precisely

      always. .

      *

Childhood—
the baby

I held
in my arms

is taller
than I

ever
dreamed.

Do no harm! This is the rule
for doctors.

We should all think of ourselves
as doctors caring for this sick world.

If we can't all be healers, at least
we can *Do no harm!*

       ★

How do you make a cloth out of thin air?
Flint and stone make a spark,

thin air catches fire. Wrap yourself up,
it's going to be a long winter.

       ★

*The red thread of passion between our legs
cannot be severed.*

Ain't that the truth? What better way to ask,
Who am I?

and not need, not want,
but know?

Snared by a line drawn in the earth,
how does one penetrate but not pass?

These bones are the lines.
I eat and drink, weep and laugh,

till the bones line up

⭐

At the seashore, count the sand, now stand
on the point of a needle.

My father drove to the ocean
to see the hurricanes first-hand.

I was born on the point of a needle
stuck in sand.

⭐

There is not one human being who doesn't
love a hot meal and a hot lover.

The kingdom of heaven is spread upon the earth
but people do not see it.

Startled by exquisite birdsong this morning—
could it have been more profound

had I known the name of the bird,
its color, size and shape?

        ★

Afternoon spent
playing jazz and blues piano.

My fingers, my arms
are feathers falling—

the price of admission:
as always, this body.

        ★

The body tells
its own story:

the wind
in the trees

breathes
a crow.

These clothes I take off
and put on each day.

Even naked, the wrinkles
and lines *caw caw caw*—

Just one part
of the story.

★

5 a.m.—my sweet wife
snores while I caress her.

To see that face
I've loved so long

sound asleep
as I rub her belly,

kiss her cheek, leave
to light the candles.

★

Whenever it thundered
my mother said the rosary.

Hard rain, a flash of lightning
and the walls rumble.

Whenever it thunders I hear
the rosary of the rain.

Doors locked, lights out,
son asleep, covers drawn—

what has been this day
has been spun into a dream.

Blessed am I to lie down
beside she who loves me.

⋆

*Why can't the master cut
the red thread of desire?*

Dharmakaya is always
giving birth—how

does she do it? Home
is where the orgasm is.

⋆

*Why can't the master speak
without using his tongue?*

When the tongue moves,
who is it who speaks?

If a "master" is there,
he's no crow.

Even the most powerful master
can't lift his legs, why?

If he's such a powerful master
there's no need to—

coming and going, birth and death
sit on his lap.

        ★

I paid for my robes,
they were not given to me.

I have no certificate,
therefore nothing to burn

except this flesh, these bones
on the cushion.

This house I've built—
paintings and poems,

sooner or later
all will be gone,

and then?

Someone else
will brew coffee

in this kitchen.

⋆

Valley Treasure Hermitage—
unlock the door in the dark

light the candles on the altar
for whatever's left of my life.

⋆

A long time ago
I grabbed his robes and said,

What makes you a Zen master,
why these robes, why this chanting?

Everyday I chant
and wear these robes.

The Eastern Garden
where rocks hold the dew

and sunlight, moonlight,
fill what's empty—

Old Crow fills
my empty cup.

★

What's true—we all get tired,
feel wasted.

What's true—we all wake up
till we don't.

Here and there, it's true —
we get to love, madly!

★

When I see a beautiful young woman

I am Mayakovsky's *cloud in trousers—*

I smile, and get blown away.

Getting old,
tired, skinny—

an in-grown toenail
reminds me

I'm here
in the kingdom of heaven.

★

Night comes
the day is fulfilled

and words fail.

Morning comes—

instant coffee,
honey on my tongue.

★

With only myself
to answer to

my chatter's
a donkey braying,

seeing not,
trudging anyway.

In my most
solitary moments

I spread my arms
out wide

with nothing
whatsoever

to say to those
I love the most.

★

Theory upon theory—
to be loved, and hated—

In the beginning was the Word.

When night comes
it's good to lie down

with the beloved
who couldn't care less.

To go home—

not a place
nor a moment,

not a word
nor a few—

dem bones,
dem bones.

★

Our shadows become slime—
Dante said so.

Whoever sees
will become soil that others

tread upon
sooner or later—

woods
lit yellow, pink,

red, brown,
black.

Think of every night
going to bed

as entering
your coffin

every night

a chance
to practice

dying.

*

I didn't start out
to paint a landscape

but the more I look
the more I feel

the heat
of the sun,

the shrill
of the breeze

climbing
the blue mountain

where my sweat
freezes.

End of day—who drinks not
gains not the *one pause.*

Music, jug wine,
a cigar on the porch—

inside and outside
birds and bugs,

bass and drums.

*

Treetops fat
with moonlight

shaken
by the insect breeze—

the wind sighs,
the curtains fly.

My wife sleeps—
the soil breathes.

The Buddha's world
is the Devil's world too.

My bliss will end in death.
Like sex. Glad to be spent.

Old slippers—drunk and divine
one by one step at a time.

      *

Climbing through trees
with razor-blade branches,

hiking across a field
where swords of grass clash;

at the top of the mountain
frigid wind makes me shiver—

my shaved pate
burned by the sun.

The face melts
like a candle.

The body
is the incense

that changes
from smoke

to pure scent.

Draft without end—
the breeze

that seasons
all things:

ablaze.

It's not what man does,
it's what a man creates.
                    —Baudelaire

To move, to age
is to make.

To be born
is to move,

to age
and make.

Surgery
is inevitable.

Mythos—Greek.

To make
a sound

with the mouth.

I shit and offer it to Buddha
　　　　—Ikkyu

What more?
It feels good

to be empty,
to be clean

like clean sheets—

If I'm going to dream
let me dream

on the clothesline.

　　　　*

Whatever truth there is
a million lies say

it isn't so. Rinzai
rattled his sleeves,

walked away.
One shout

says all there is
to say.

Beyond that
it's all fiction.

The triple world
is right here,

Not two, not one.
Not many.

When I lower
my eyes

and breathe,
my body

still as stone:
Where does time go?

When time comes,
I ring the bell.

In a landslide
        of stones

I found
        the skeleton

of a crow—
        bones

picked clean,
            scattered;

feathers gone
            in the scree.

Dem Bones

They shiver
            from cold.

The room
            gets smaller.

The body
            gets smaller.

They shiver
            from cold.

This world

has always
 been

a small
 one.

Dem bones.

NOTES

"Tokudo Shiki"—The name of the ordination ceremony of Zen monks. *Tokudo* means "To grasp the wisdom of the enlightened." *Shiki means* "Ceremony."

ACKNOWLEDGEMENTS

Thanks to the following magazines, where some of these poems first appeared: *Agni, The Iowa Review, La Bella Figura, The New Review, North Dakota Quarterly, Ploughshares, Prairie Schooner, Rattle,* and the *Rocky Mountain Review.*

I'd like to express my gratitude to Stephen Berg for his wonderful translation of Ikkyu's poems "Crow With No Mouth." I have always felt that these translations capture the spirit of Ikkyu in a way that others don't. To Stephen Berg, a deep gassho. SRR

green
press
INITIATIVE